BARBARA BEARE

Winning the Tug of War that is Human Resources

Practical tips for the HR Professional to navigate the tug of war between employees and employers.

First edition

This book was professionally typeset on Reedsy.
Find out more at reedsy.com

Contents

1

Chapter 1

Introduction

The purpose of this book is to make the journey easier for those relatively new to the field of Human Resources and help you navigate future interactions with employees and employers.

So, you want to be an HR professional. We all get into HR because we truly like to help people. We spend time studying our craft, learning best practices, and keeping up to date on employment laws and government regulations, merely to name a few. Then, we continuously follow up on new developments, attend seminars, and educate ourselves on best practices. We are a strategic partner helping to drive the business forward, limit liability, and prevent lawsuits, all while creating a positive work environment. The job should come with a superhero cape.

Court decisions, new legislation, mergers and acquisitions, changes in ownership, etc. can change and we are tasked with navigating all of it. Sometimes that means siding with the employee's perspective and sometimes that means siding with the leadership's perspective.

Communication with leadership and employees can create a lot of angst on both sides.

Interestingly, when you sit down to have these conversations, they are often based on facts and information learned by a change in some area of the human resource field yet for some reason, the owners of the company believe that the only reason you've brought the subject up is because you're always on the employee's side. Or at least that is the feedback I have often been given. Conversely, if you need to explain to employees a new policy, based on a change in the laws or best practices, they believe that HR is doing it merely because you're always on the company's side. Don't allow either side to pull you into their negativity. You are just doing your job.

I have been in HR for more than 20 years and I can't tell you how many times I have allowed myself to feel stuck in the middle. Did you notice, I used the words "allowed myself"? Please remember that neither side can pull you into their negative opinion unless you allow them to.

This is also true when it comes to turnover rates. Companies don't understand that their culture and management style often create turnover. They expect HR to find ways to make the employees want to stay through employee engagement. Friday's fun day or an occasional free lunch will not make up for a toxic environment. How can we do that if the company isn't willing to look at their compensations, benefits, management style, etc? We are not miracle workers.

This book will not give you an A-to-Z breakdown of every human resource best practice nor is it intended to. It does not contain scholarly research or other expert advice. Let's be real—HR is difficult to execute, and we don't always have the time to read a long how-to book. This book is meant to be a quick read to share practical tips I have learned to help navigate both the employee's and employer's needs. Tips that will help you understand what is most important from the employee and the employer's perspective when you cannot completely, please either side.

The first four chapters will illustrate some of the experiences that led me to the conclusions I will share with you from the employee and employer perspectives. The stories are real, but some facts and names have been modified for privacy reasons. So don't look up the companies I have worked for, get out your pitchforks and stage a revolt. Telling these stories will help set the stage for understanding the remaining chapters where we will dive into the lessons I have learned. I learned many of these tips the hard way.

The next chapter will dive into the employee's point of view. With such a diverse and unique group of individuals in one setting, you will find many different perspectives and interpretations of the world around them. This includes how they look at employment practices and choose to interpret the policies and procedures of a company. I have learned that no amount of coaching and mentoring can get some people to "get out of their own way". In a perfect world, we could stop bad behavior before it happens. Is that possible with so many different points of view? Maybe not but, there are things beyond training, coaching, and mentoring that could help and we will look at them in this chapter.

Next, we will look at how best to handle communications with leadership. Even though it is in your job description to mitigate risk, limit liability, and the unwritten rule—keep them out of lawsuits. These conversations can be tricky when the leadership's ideas and opinions on the subject don't align with that outcome. Your job security is in their hands. You have bills to pay and mouths to feed. Fear may give you pause when needed to have tough conversations. The biggest thing I have learned is they need choices. "Because it is the Law" may seem like a strong argument; however, it never goes over well.

I hope my experiences and the stories I shared will help you better navigate the often-thankless job of the HR professional.

2

Chapter 2

New Laws Can Be a Challenge

Sometimes government regulation causes us to get stuck in the middle. In 2013, I read a rule in an article that came out through one of my HR subscriptions regarding the Affordable Care Act. One of the new regulations was that beginning January 1, 2014, employers must now offer health insurance coverage to any employee working over 30 hours a week. Employers would now have many more people taking advantage of health insurance benefits if they were part-time employees even if the employer's policies were not to offer benefits to part-time employees.

At the time, I worked for a company with a large percentage of part-time employees, and of those part-time employees at least half worked 30 hours or more a week. Quickly crunching some numbers, this meant quite a large increase in expense.

During our regular weekly meeting, I explained the Affordable Care Act to the owners and what that would mean for us going forward. I was immediately met with hostility as if I personally wrote and put this new act in place just to piss them off. This was often how they responded. If you work for leadership such as this, the most important skill to have is emotional intelligence. It is important to understand that these reactions are not about you, the HR professional. They are about leadership feeling out of control of a situation. Keeping that in mind, I quickly jumped to an obvious solution. Part-time employees are not allowed to work more than 30 hours a week.

This meant we could not schedule anyone for 30 hours either because that was the level at which we would have to offer insurance. Anyone who has ever done payroll knows that when employees punch in early or punch out late, even by just a minute, the result would push someone over the 30 hours.

After some discussion, the decision was made to make the maximum hours allowed per week be set at 28 that way should they go over slightly? They would still be under the 30-hour maximum to keep us in compliance. Additionally, they decided not to be transparent with the employees and did not disclose it was because we did not want to provide health insurance for part-time people. The presentation should merely be sold as a change in company policy. I disagreed with this course of action. Transparency is the best policy as it yields trust. Sometimes you must pick your battles.

The next step in the process was getting 30 different managers together to explain the new regulations and the reasons behind the company's decision. Although they understood there was some grumbling. Keep in mind that this is now going to require more oversight on their part. For example, if one team member fell ill and couldn't work their scheduled shift, they could call around and get their shift covered by another team member. The manager did not mind if the shift was covered. This would no longer be possible. The manager must now monitor the changes to keep everyone under 30 hours. In addition, they will no longer be able to give premium hours to their best producers and what will that mean for their numbers? Fear of the unknown is a big obstacle for the management team.

Because the regulation would take effect in January 2014, and the owners did not want employees to know they didn't wish to offer part-time employees health insurance, the decision was made to sell it as a change in company policy. I suggested that since we had some other necessary updates to the handbook, we just update it for a January 2014 release. This seemed logical, so we agreed to create a new version of the handbook for everybody to read and sign. As all HR professionals know, handbooks should be looked at regularly and updated so this makes the most sense. The owners agreed.

As the time neared, we had a video conference with all the part-time employees with the topic being- Handbook Changes. Each manager brought their teams into the conference room at their prospective offices, put the meeting up on the big screen, and logged into the meeting. Human Resources presented it from the Corporate Office.

We had prepared a PowerPoint with each slide containing an upcoming change in the handbook. This included things we added, changed, and or deleted from the current edition of the handbook. We requested everyone keep questions for the end and proceeded with the meeting.

The owners were under the assumption that no one would ask about the Affordable Care Act or the 30-hour rule and that could not have been further from the truth. Keep in mind that it only took one person bringing it up to now open the eyes of the other 400-plus employees on the call. The question went something like this. Does the implementation of a maximum number of hours part-time employees can work have anything to do with that new law stating employers must now offer us health insurance if we work 30 hours? You could immediately hear the reaction from employees. "What new law?" "Do you have to offer us health insurance now?" "If I don't want health insurance, can I still work more than 30 hours?" My fear was realized. Having the truth come out this way breeds mistrust in the company and leadership. And more importantly, employees group HR in the same bucket as leadership when things like this happen.

In the coming weeks, you guessed, "stuck in the middle". Each side had their feeling about the subject. When we cannot convince leadership to go in another direction, in this case, be transparent. All we can do is walk out of the meeting and present a unified front that we are on board with the decision. Like it or not, this is the job. We work for the company. But be prepared because employees take their frustration out on HR. You begin to feel that employees believe that every HR professional wakes up in the morning and says to themselves, "How can I upset everyone today?" Let me say that I know that most HR professionals reading this book can relate to this feeling. We do this job because we truly want to help people. We do not make the laws and yet somehow the fingers are often pointing, and the tongues are often waging in our direction.

3

Chapter 3

Disability and Accommodation Conflict

We often get stuck in the middle merely because one side or the other cannot get out of their own way. When one owns a business and provides jobs for many people, they should be commended. It's an amazing accomplishment. And even though the business is yours that does not mean you have no one to answer to but yourself. This is why you hire an HR professional, their expertise is in laws regulations, best practices, etc. to limit liability and lawsuits.

I returned to work after vacation to find that my recruiter had hired several new line workers. I took the time to meet with them to welcome them to the company in person. One of the individuals reminded me a lot of my nephew who is on the autism spectrum, we will call her, Amanda. A week after Amanda started, the VP of Operations, we will call him Fred, was in my office telling me that Amanda came into his office to let him know her job coach would be coming to the plant later that week to observe her at work. She stated it was due to her disability. Naturally, he was taken by surprise since he had no knowledge of a disability, but he kept his composure and thanked her for bringing it to his attention. He told her he would talk to HR and get back to her with the next steps.

Fred came to my office, explained what had happened, and asked why he was not told. My response was that I did not know anything about it either. We immediately reached out to the recruiter and Fred shared with him that Amanda stated she told him about having a disability during her interview. The recruiter said nothing was ever mentioned. I asked Fred to go back to his notes and he confirmed there was nothing in the notes.

Upon speaking to Amanda, she said she did bring it up during her interview and was told to let us know during onboarding. But you did not bring it up during onboarding Amanda because I was the one who did your onboarding. I explained that we would now have to start the interactive process. The process revealed that she was in fact on the autism spectrum.

For those who have never had an interaction with someone on the spectrum, some things that may be present; they often get overstimulated, they are sensitive to noise, they communicate very bluntly and can offend people without meaning to, and they don't always understand how to take things that are said to them. These were all true in her case. We sat down with her job coach and agreed to a plan of action to include sitting down with all the floor supervisors to explain the need for accommodation and how they could help. We also agreed to extra short breaks for when she got overstimulated and higher decibel earplugs for sound.

The owner of the company was informed by the VP of Operations that we had hired someone on the autism spectrum, so he immediately came to see me. I explained to him that we engaged in the interactive process, what we learned, and how we were moving forward to accommodate. His thoughts were quite the opposite. He had concerns about our regulations which would not permit the job coach on the production floor. I explained that we were not allowing the coach on the floor but had a different solution in mind. He did not want to permit her to take extra breaks with valid reason and questioned the noise-canceling earplugs requested. I assured him we were providing the right course of action and explained the Americans with Disabilities Act (ADA), and that my goal was to keep us out of a lawsuit.

Over the next month, we worked with Amanda to accommodate her needs. Although our operations did not allow outsiders to be on the plant floor, we invited her job coach to sit down with all the supervisors so we could discuss how to accommodate Amanda, and how to best communicate with her and understand her communication style. During that meeting, we learned of many tall tales Amanda had been telling. The supervisors were concerned it was creating an unproductive work environment.

We were also told that Amanda was abusing the extra break time. She stayed out for excessive periods during each break. Shortly after the reports of the stories Amanda was telling became much more grandiose and included a lot of untrue and misinformation. I am not going to go into details, but let's just say the behaviors were disturbing and beyond the scope of accommodation for a disability. That said, we were trying our best to work through the special needs and make her successful.

While all this was happening, I was visited by the owner of the company again who wanted me to get rid of her. I explained to him that we were doing our best to investigate all reports. We had not found any witnesses to any of the accusations. Without witnesses, we could not move forward with any disciplinary action. My hands were tied. All he heard was that I was going against his wishes. Anyone who has been in HR for any amount of time I'm sure can cite a similar story where HR is trying to keep the company out of a lawsuit and have only good intentions by moving slowly and ensuring that everything is done correctly and yet somehow, we are looked at as public enemy number one by the owners for doing so. I liken it to pulling the owner out of the way of a speeding train just before it hits them and having them be upset with you for the resulting bruise on their arm.

Unfortunately, the story ended with the employee getting terminated for cause as one of the investigations did reveal wrongdoing.

4

Chapter 4

Top Performer

But he is my top performer. Has anybody ever heard that before? For some reason, there is a widely held belief amongst company owners that if the individual is a top performer the rules can't possibly apply to them. This has been true in many companies where I have worked.

I once worked for a company that found out that one of our top sales performers, David, who also happened to be in management, was involved in a major legal battle where he was accused of scamming money, to the tune of millions of dollars, with other individuals. David was on an in-home sales call when the customer recognized his name. She immediately called into our office to ask us if we knew the type of person we had working for us and shared the story. We immediately entered his name and searched online. An article came up, confirming everything she had shared.

At this company, there were four owners. The story quickly spread through the halls of the building. Sitting down with the owners to discuss the next steps I discovered they were already aware of David's legal issues. Because David was a top performer, they decided to allow David to continue working while the situation was being adjudicated. I could not believe my ears.

Have you ever contracted to have someone do work in your house? As a precaution, the company will give you the name of who to expect. I always look them up. My immediate reaction was to explain to the owners that I wouldn't let anybody in my house without looking them up to ensure they were not a threat. If I came across this, I would wonder what kind of company would employ him and I wouldn't want to do business with them. Not to mention the elephant in the room. Now everyone knows about David after the customer called into the main line to share her concerns. What kind of message will be sent to the other employees if we allow David to continue working? My recommendation was to let him go! An unpopular one to say the least. I was accused of never giving them any choices. At the time, I didn't understand what other choice there was.

David did end up getting convicted and going to prison.

5

Chapter 5

Relatives

Whether you are working at a family-owned company or for a company without a strong nepotism policy, challenges of family working together are bound to happen. At a relatively small family-owned company, we had an individual who had severe allergic reactions to most scents. We will call her Sally. She would break out into hives, not be able to breathe, get severe headaches, and other violent health reactions when exposed. This often caused her to remove herself from the facility and kept her from performing her job.

I learned of her debilitating condition shortly after I started. Sally had called me to report a strong smell in the building. She wasn't sure what it was, but she needed to walk outside to get some fresh air. I walked out to her work area and immediately smelled what seemed to be an air freshener. This is when she shared with me her extreme allergic condition and pleaded for my help. She had been dealing with this for quite some time before my starting with the company. I asked her if she knew who was doing it and she would not tell me. All she would say is that it was someone high up and she feared for her job by exposing them.

Having allergic reactions to flowers and scents myself, I completely empathize with her. She shared with me that our handbook had a section about strong perfumes and colognes, but nothing else. I sat down with executive management to explain the problem, and the first reaction I got was, "Sally complains about everything." Being new to the company I had no knowledge of Sally's history however I shared this is a health condition. We have no choice, but to accommodate under the ADA.

After some discussion, I was given the support to rewrite the policy to include not only perfumes and colognes, but any, and all scented items including air fresheners, candles, plug-ins, etc. I immediately wrote a new policy, created a memo to disseminate to the team and sent it to everybody via email and posted it on the dashboard of our HRIS system. After doing so we went around, gathered up all the company purchased air fresheners and disposed of them.

Immediately afterwards, the brother of the owner, we will call him Tom, came to me very upset. He said that air fresheners are necessary to neutralize the odors in the restrooms. I did not find this a compelling argument. Let's be real, air fresheners do not neutralize the odor in the restrooms. Once sprayed, you merely smell shit and flowers all at the same time. He then shared that he also believes Sally to be a complainer, but when I shared with him that I too reacted negatively, too strongly scented items he had no rebuttal. I suggested we find a non-scented alternative that can neutralize odors and not merely try to mask them. He nodded in agreement and left my office.

A couple of days later, Sally reached out to me and said there's a very strong odor here. I do not know where it's coming from. We investigated

16

and found certain individuals from Tom's team were bringing in their own air freshener and spraying it anyway. Do you remember the game, Follow the Leader, from when you were young? That does not change when you are all grown up. People follow their leader. In this case, the leader disagreed with the new policy and turned a blind eye to his direct reports following the policy.

It is a slippery slope when you are going up against a relative of the owner so calling them out directly is not a solution. Instead, I sent the memo again with an explanation stating that we now had a NO scents policy due to severe allergic reactions from some team members. This time we included verbiage that we know nobody would want to purposely make their coworkers ill and that we appreciate their cooperation. What happened next?

You guessed it, she reached out again. I walked into the restroom and could smell the strong odor but had no idea where it was coming from so, I started looking behind things, under things, and found air fresheners like you put in the car. You know the ones shaped like trees. They were tied up underneath the sinks. Because I was new to the company, and Tom was the owner's brother, I felt I needed advice on how to navigate the problem. I shared this with my boss who immediately removed them.

Not much time had passed until Sally was sitting at her desk, covered in hives as my boss walked by. He asked her if she was all right and she said no the smell coming from the bathroom is making me ill. He went in to discover hidden air fresheners again and immediately removed them. My boss then shared with me that Tom came into his office enraged that we would merely remove the air fresheners without even a discussion with him. Seriously! Your coworker is near hospitalization due to a medical condition she cannot control and all you care about is your right to have an air freshener in the bathroom.

If just any employee would have done this, they would've been terminated for insubordination on the spot. After all this directive came down from the owner of the company. Thankfully, the well-being of the employees was a priority for the owner who stood by the policy regardless of his brother's complaints and continued to be non-compliant. That said, it does nothing for employee morale and trust in an employer when good people watch bad behavior being allowed. Refusing to hold a family member to the same standard as everyone else will cause unnecessary turnover or at the very least Quiet Quitting.

6

Chapter 6

The Employee perspective – How to win them over

The previous three chapters were meant to set the stage for how unimaginable things happen at work. I used to have a running joke with an owner of a company I worked for who would often say to me, "Just when you thought you had enough material for the book you want to write" after most of our interactions. That was many years ago and I was not the only one having the same idea. Recently I saw a book titled *You can't make this shit up*. That would have been exactly what I would have called my book had I ever gotten around to writing it. Trust me, if you are new to the HR profession, you will soon understand that statement and, if you are a seasoned professional reading this book to get some shared insight, you will completely relate.

Let's start by admitting the truth that most employees do not want to hear – HR is NOT your friend. Yes, we care and are friendly, but HR professionals need to be experts at drawing the line between personal relationships with co-workers and doing their job. It is a balance that can make you feel stuck in the middle if you become too emotionally involved with your co-workers. That may sound harsh, but this is emotional intelligence.

If you want to survive in HR, hell if you want to survive in life, you need emotional intelligence. No this is not something you are born with; it is something you learn and develop over time. Most people could do more to develop this skill. Invest in a book or coaching session on the subject. It will be well worth the investment of time and money. Especially if you are in HR because being an HR professional means you need to be able to separate personal from professional.

I once worked closely with a girl I thought the world of as a person; however, I was not fond of her work ethic. We will call her Anne. Anne was let go for not meeting the company's expectations. Honestly, it was the right decision, and I was 100% on board with letting her go. During the discussion leading up to her separation, I even provided reasons from a performance and budgetary aspect that led to the outcome.

Afterward, we would meet for drinks, and I am still in contact with her more than a decade later. Why? As an HR professional, you need to be able to separate your feelings about the person from your feelings about the employee. They are two different people in the HR world. She understood that I was doing my job, and it wasn't personal. Why? Because she had emotional intelligence.

Another harsh reality is HR does not fire people; they fire themselves. It is merely our job to facilitate their walk out the door. If we let ourselves get emotionally involved in this, we would spend our days in a therapist's office and not the HR office.

Let us get down to business—What can we do to help employees understand that we are on their side even if we sometimes agree with the company? First, always keep an open mind, everyone views things from their unique perspective. I cannot describe this any better than Allen Mallory did in his February 2020 post where he discusses how our unique perspectives on life and how we approach and perceive things directly relate to our upbringing, education, experiences, and personality. In other words, be open to new perspectives. This does not mean you have to agree or that the employee's perspective will result in any change but showing you care enough to hear them out is a great first step in improving employee relations.

Additionally, the employee may have read the policy and understood it in a way it may not have been intended. Allow them to describe to you how they interpreted the meaning of the policy. You may find that you can completely understand how they could have inferred that meaning even though you know that was not the original intent of the policy. Who knows, the employee's perspective could lead to a larger discussion and a change in policy that is better suited for everyone. I have seen this happen. At the very least, some necessary tweaking of the wording of the policy may make for better clarification moving forward. This practice is called active listening.

Active listening is a skill that will serve you well not only with employee interactions but will do wonders for your personal relationships as well. I must admit, this was an area where I needed work. One of the daily tasks of HR is to solve people's problems. For example, if someone can't log into the payroll system, they stop by your office and as the HR professional, you put on your Superman cape or Wonder Woman bracelets and help them out. So, my natural instinct when someone stopped by my office was to listen to them for a moment and jump in with my solution. I am wearing my Wonder Woman bracelets after all.

This is not what the employees want. They want someone who will allow them to speak and show that they are completely listening. This is done by allowing the employee to tell their story, no matter how long it takes. You must resist the urge to butt into the conversation and merely wait for them to finish. While they are talking, you should keep eye contact and ensure your body language is open and you are nodding your head in understanding. Keep your facial expressions positive and interject with an "uh huh" to show you are hearing them. If you believe you would benefit from learning more about active listening, there are a plethora of resources out there or you could consider a communication coach.

The next skill is empathy. Empathy comes naturally to most people when dealing with their inner circle, but people have a harder time relating to someone whose background or perspective is different than their own. This is why keeping an open mind and active listening were explained first. To empathize with someone, you must first seek to understand them, where they are in that moment. Back when I first got in the workforce, what I would hear most often from employers was "leave your personal stuff at the door–this is work". As we all know, that is easier said than done. What is going on outside of work will often affect our mood or ability to be at our best at work.

One of the things the pandemic did positively for society, in my opinion, is to open our eyes to that fact. The anxiety caused by the Pandemic made many not want to return to traditional on-site working arrangements due to the fear of becoming ill. This anxiety also kept people from going to a store, a restaurant, or other public places. The isolation led to depression, and many are still suffering the effects today. Opening everyone's eyes to the importance of mental health was long overdue in the workplace.

Be intentional, understand that whatever is going on with the person sitting across from you is the most important thing to them at that moment. As an HR professional, you may have five or six different things to complete, and you may not really think their problem is all that big—It is to them. Be empathetic.

In the first chapter, we discussed a policy change based on the government passing the 30-hour rule. It would have been easy to throw our hands in the air and say—it is the government's fault—complain to them. As you recall, the employees were not focused on the new rule, they were focused on the company's decision not to allow anyone to go over 30 hours. The focus was on the offering of health insurance.

In this situation, even though I kept an open mind, listened, and empathized, none of that would change the company's decision. This leads us to the fourth suggestion, listen to feedback and take action on it. It is never good when a large faction of your workforce is upset.

It was time to think outside the box and brainstorm a proposal that may work for both sides.

Approximately 10 percent of the part-time workforce were very high performers, so we typically allowed them to work hours very close to being full-time. That led to a discussion with a team of stakeholders about how badly we wanted our valuable employees to stay and what we could do to make that happen. We reviewed the hours needed in each area and utilized data analytics to reveal the underperformers who should be let go. We compiled everyone's ideas and feedback and implemented a full-time position for that department for the first time. Naturally, it was only offered to those top-performing individuals and was a great way to get those who may not have been performing as well as they could have something to strive for, creating a win-win. When employers show that they are listening by implementing something new based on employee feedback, the goodwill earned is unmeasurable.

One last thing to keep in mind regarding employee feedback. Many companies like to send out employee surveys on various topics as an easy way to get employee feedback. A word of caution, if you do a survey, you must also follow up. The worst thing an employer can do is send out a survey and then do nothing with the information they receive. For example, if you ask employees what type of social activities, they would like to see the company do and then don't do any social activities suggested this will cause a larger negative reaction than never taking the time to get their opinions in the first place.

7

Chapter 7

The Employer Perspective

In my experience, employers hate to be told they have no choices. If you recall, in chapter two we told the story of Amanda, the young lady we hired who was on the autism spectrum. HR professionals are very in tune with the ADA. We are well versed in engaging in the interactive process to determine if accommodation is necessary and available without it being a hardship to the company. There isn't a lot of gray there. When leadership told me to get rid of her, they didn't like hearing that wasn't an option. Moreover, they also had some colorful suggestions on how to arrange her accommodations. None of which I was particularly comfortable with.

Being aware from previous experience that owners require HR professionals to think outside the box to ensure the outcome they want whenever possible, my response went something like this. If we get rid of her, we get sued, if we don't give her the reasonable accommodations she requested, we get sued. The third option is, to follow the interactive process and see what happens. Knowing the reaction that was coming, I felt I needed to give them information they would perceive as positive. I then shared that Amanda had not been following the accommodation agreement regarding her extra five-minute breaks. It is important to understand that not having enough people at each machine meant the machine couldn't run causing production to halt. Amanda was taking 20 and 30-minute breaks. I explained that being patient and allowing us to coach and document could lead to termination for cause.

Although these choices may not have been the immediate outcome leadership was looking for, because I presented it in this way, leadership did not feel they were being told what to do giving them the respect to choose on their own. Respect is the golden ticket when dealing with owners and leadership.

What do the stories about Amanda in chapter two and David in chapter three have in common? My main focus was to keep us out of a lawsuit. Trust me when I say leadership and owners expect their HR professionals to limit liability and prevent lawsuits. After reading both chapters, one might shake their head at this expectation. Creating a positive work environment for employees and navigating the opportunities that present themselves from employee behavior isn't the only thing we must look out for. Employers often create just as many opportunities on their side of the equation.

David was clearly a liability for the company and yet leadership couldn't see past the dollars he generated. The worst part about that example was that they knew and kept it quiet. In the last example, the owner allowed his brother to create a hostile, unproductive work environment and continue leading a team in the company without ever documenting the incident. Now we will never know what conversations they had behind closed doors. But does that matter? From an employee's perspective if my boss doesn't care about this policy; it must not be important.

Therefore, I do not need to care about it or follow it. When we allow employees not to follow the smallest of policies, it makes some believe they don't need to follow any of the policies they deem unnecessary. This is a bad precedent to set.

I chose these examples to demonstrate how as HR professionals we face impossible situations that put us in the line of fire and they are often at the hands of leadership and not the employees. As HR professionals, we expect leadership to follow the rules they put in place, but that does not always happen. Many have the 'my way or the highway' mentality and want to pick and choose who the rules apply to.

The best suggestion I can give you is this. Explain to the owners that the policies in their handbook are their policies. Is not that a profound statement? Leadership often forgets that they created or approved the policies. and that if they don't wish to follow a policy, then get rid of it. Not consistently following the rules with everyone, all the time will eventually get them into hot water. Another option would be to simply reword a policy so it more closely aligns with the company's mission. But most importantly—do away with policies they no longer believe serve their vision. This will solve many problems and keep HR from being stuck in the middle.

Anytime an HR professional needs to address leadership, they must do it respectfully. Showing respect is not an option when dealing with humans—it is a necessity! Even when you view leadership's actions as wrong. Or let's take that one step further, when there is no doubt they are out of their minds, you must approach the conversation with respect. I am sure you have been told, how you say something makes all the difference. Albert Mehrabian coined the phrase "it is not what you say but how you say it" in the 1970's. This is a phrase I repeat often and truly believe. Ensure you approach every communication with leadership respectfully, even when you are on opposite sides of the issue.

Throughout the examples limiting liability and keeping the company out of lawsuits is the job of HR professionals, this is expected even while balancing, recruiting, onboarding, employee engagement, benefit administration, payroll, strategic planning, training, and development, and we could go on and on. The list of expectations for an HR professional is long; however, keep your focus on the things that matter most to the leadership in your company to be successful. I have learned you can accomplish 5000 things in a day, but if you did not accomplish the one thing leadership values the most, you accomplished nothing. Keep the channels of communication open.

8

Chapter 8

Conclusion

Being an HR professional isn't for the faint of heart. We must be able to appease both the employee and the employer even when neither side is necessarily getting what they want. Changes in the legal landscape, leadership changes, policy changes, and even a lack of emotional intelligence could be responsible. Sometimes there is no good outcome, there are only possibilities and choices.

The best we can do is make employees feel valued, always keep an open mind, practice active listening, be empathetic, and do your very best to take the employee's feedback and take some action on it. Taking action shows that your employees matter to you and studies have shown that when employees feel valued, they will work harder. In 2012, an APA survey showed if an employee felt valued they also had better well-being.

When it comes to employers, remember to provide them with choices. Most do not like a black-and-white mentality. They want you to at least present it with some gray. This may require thinking outside the box to provide an additional solution that may bend the rules but doesn't go as far as breaking them.

Always speak to leadership respectfully even when you want to scream—WTF! And remember regardless of whether they are standing in the way, they expect you to limit their liability and keep them out of lawsuits. The best way to keep yourself from getting stuck from the employer's perspective is communication. Insist on regular 1:1's with leadership or ask for a seat at the table. Communication is key.

One of my favorite quotes is by George Bernard Shaw ' The trouble with communication, is the illusion that it has taken place." Ask clarifying questions to ensure you understand the needs of both employees and employers.

I hope my experiences and advice will serve you in your HR career. If you found this book helpful and informative, please leave a favorable review on Amazon. Thank you and God Bless!

Citations

[Communication Coach Alexander Lyon]. (2020, June 16). *Active Listening Skills* [Video]. YouTube. https://youtu.be/7wUCyjiyXdg

APA survey finds feeling valued at work linked to Well-Being and performance. (2012). [Dataset]. In *PsycEXTRA Dataset.* https://doi.org/10.1037/e601812012-001

Mowery, A. (2020, February 6). *How Our Unique Perspectives Make a Team Stronger.* Alanmowery.com. Retrieved June 7, 2024, from https://alanmallory.com/2020/02/how-our-unique-perspectives-make-a-team-stronger

Dunbar, R. (2022, January 7). *It's not what you say but how you say it.* Society for Personal and Social Psychology. Retrieved June 7, 2024, from https://spsp.org/news-center/character-context-blog/its-not-what-you-say-its-how-you-say-it